Spelling Practice

Exercises devised by Brenda Apsley
an experienced author and editor who specialises
in writing early learning books for children
Illustrated by John Haslam

Learning Rewards is a home-learning programme designed to help your child succeed at school with the National Curriculum. It has been extensively researched with parents and teachers.

This book, *Spelling Practice*, and its companion title, *Spelling Skills*, cover important aspects of the National Curriculum at Key Stage I.

Children should start with the *Skills* books (with younger children this is important) and progress to the *Practice* books.

The *Skills* book teaches basic skills and new concepts through structured and enjoyable activities. The *Practice* book reinforces and builds on these skills by the essential repetition of exercises.

You will need to work through each page with your child and talk about what is required. The star symbol at the top of the page details the particular skills covered by the exercise as they relate to the National Curriculum. The content is progressive, so explain the importance of starting from the front of the book.

When you come to the end of the book you will find a progress chart. This is a useful record of your child's performance.

Always reward your child's work with encouragement and a gold star sticker.

series editor: Nina Filipek series designer: Paul Dronsfield
cover illustration: Chris Simpson designer: Hilary Edwards-Malam
Copyright © 2001 Egmont Books Limited.
All rights reserved.
Published in Great Britain by
Egmont Books Limited,
239 Kensington High Street, London W8 6SA.
Printed in Italy.
ISBN 0 7498 5157 0
10 9 8 7 6 5 4 3

Spelling

First and last-letter sounds

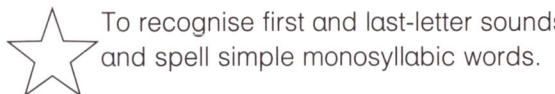 To recognise first and last-letter sounds and spell simple monosyllabic words.

Spell a word for each bee by writing in a missing letter. The missing letters are at the **start** or **end** of the words. There can be more than one right answer.

- ca_t_
- _an
- ba_
- _in
- _ig
- _et
- _it
- pi_
- di_
- an_
- li_

2

Spelling

 To recognise first and last-letter sounds and spell simple monosyllabic words.

First and last-letter sounds

_ u n

m a _

_ a t

d o _

b u _

_ o t

_ e d

c o _

_ u g

l o _

w e _

_ e n

m u _

Spelling

Words with a

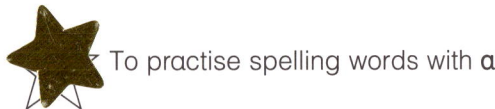
To practise spelling words with a.

Write **a** to spell the words. Spell each word three times.

h a t — hat   hat   hat
b a t — bat   bat   bat
l a m p — lamp   lamp   lamp
f l a g — flag   flag   flag
h a n d — hand   hand   band
a p p l e — apple   apple   apple

Tick the words that are spelled correctly. Spell them below.

cap ✓   van ✓   bag ✓   mat ✓
cape   varn   bap   matt

cap   van   bag   mat

Spelling

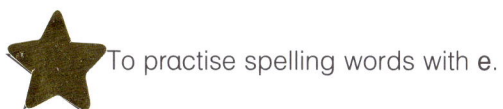
To practise spelling words with e.

Words with e

Write **e** to spell the words. Spell each word three times.

b_e_d — beb   beb   beb
h_e_n — heb   hey   heb
t_e_nt — tent   tent   tent
w_e_b — web   wep   web
p_e_n — pen   pen   pen
n_e_st — henz   nest   hect

Tick the words that are spelled correctly. Spell them below.

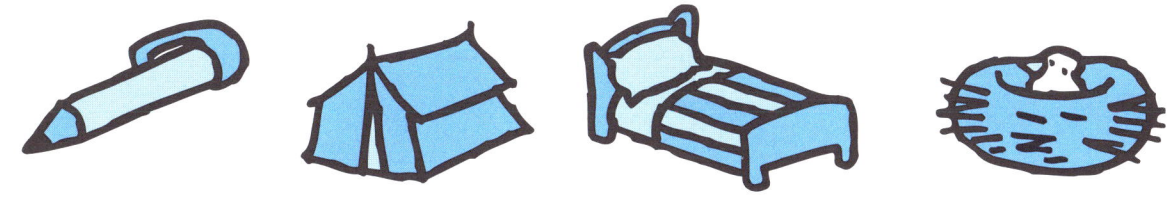

| pen | temt | beb | nest |
| penn | tent | bed | ness |

pen   tent   bed   nest

Spelling

Words with **i**, **o** and **u**

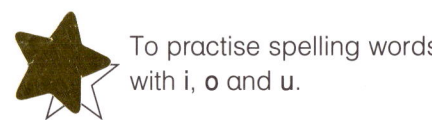
To practise spelling words with i, o and u.

Write the letters **i**, **o** or **u** to spell the words.
Spell each word three times.

s u n  sun sun sun

c o t  cot cot cot

s o c k  sock sock sock

h i ll  hill hill hill

j u g  jug jug jug

t i n  tin tin tin

m u g  mug mug mug

d o g  dog dog dog

r a b b i t  rabbit rabbit rabbit

c a r r o t carrot carrot carrot

Spelling

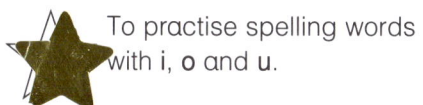
To practise spelling words with i, o and u.

Words with **i**, **o** and **u**

Rearrange the letters to spell the words correctly.
Spell each word twice more.

n u b   bun   bun   bun

g n i k   cing   cing   cing

f x o   fxo   fxo   fxo

n u r   run   run   run

g o l   log   log   log

Spell the **i**, **o** or **u** words that finish the sentences.

The box is not small. It is <u>big</u>.   bug   bag   big

I can <u>leg</u> on one leg.   hip   hop   hold

I <u>hit</u> the ball with a bat.   hit   hat   hut

In summer the <u>hot</u> is <u>sun</u>.   hot   hat   sun

7

Spelling

Words with **ck** and **st**

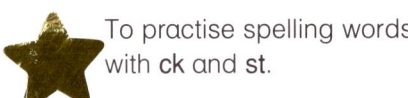 To practise spelling words with ck and st.

Choose **ck** or **st** to spell the words.
Spell the words to finish the sentences.

c h i **ck**  A baby hen is called a **chick**.

St a m p s  Anna collects **stamps**.

St a r s  The **stars** come out at night.

c l o **ck**  Tick, tock, goes the **clock**.

l i **st**  Write a **list** of things to do.

Tick the **ck** words that are spelled correctly.

| brock | ticket | lorck | sack | truck |
| brick | tikit | lock | seck | turck |

Tick the correct **st** words.

| stop | fast | larst | steck | first |
| stap | fest | last | stick | furst |

8

Spelling

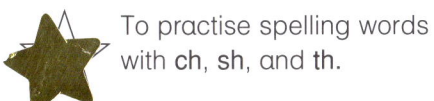

To practise spelling words with **ch**, **sh**, and **th**.

Words with **ch**, **sh**, **th**

Spell the words with **ch** and **sh** letters. Write each word twice, then cover the words. Can you spell the words on your own?

Sh o e — Shoe Shoe Shoe
ch a i r — chair chair chair
fi sh — fish fish fish
mat ch — match match match
Sh e l l — Shell Shell Shell

Underline all the words with **th** in the story below.

<u>This</u> is Joe Smith.

There are four people in the Smith family.

Joe has a brother called Tim.

Tim is older than Joe.

Tim and Joe live with their mother and father.

Spelling

Words with 'magic e'

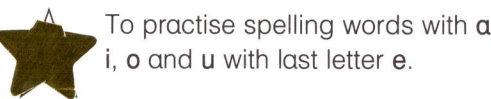
To practise spelling words with a, i, o and u with last letter e.

Add **e** to the picture words to spell new words.
Spell the **new** words.

can ____ + e = _ _ _ _

pin ____ + e = _ _ _ _

tap ____ + e = _ _ _ _

pan ____ + e = _ _ _ _

Spell each word twice, then cover and try to spell again, on your own this time. Draw lines to match the words and pictures.

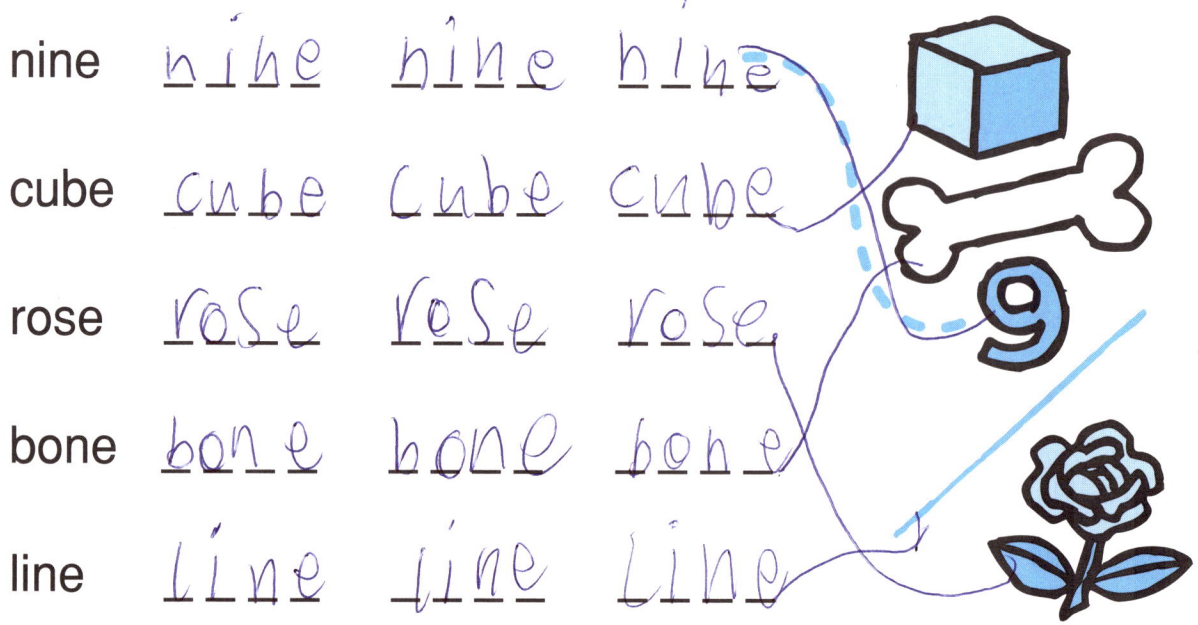

nine   nine   nine   nine

cube   cube   cube   cube

rose   rose   rose   rose

bone   bone   bone   bone

line   line   line   line

Spelling

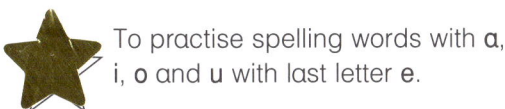

To practise spelling words with a, i, o and u with last letter e.

Words with 'magic e'

All the words in the crossword end with **e**.
Spell the words then complete the crossword.

1 l a k e = **lake**
2 p o l e = **pole**
3 k i t e = **kite**
4 p a g e = **page**
5 g a t e = **gate**
6 t a l e = **tale**
7 m o l e = **mole**
8 m i c e = **mice**

Spelling

Words with bl, cl, fl, gl, pl, sl

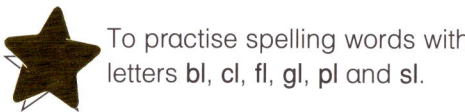
To practise spelling words with letters bl, cl, fl, gl, pl and sl.

Write the letters that spell the words.
Write **bl**, **cl**, **fl**, **gl**, **pl** or **sl**. Spell each word three times.

Slide — slide slide slide
Slate — slate slate slate
Clock — clock clock clock
flag — flag flag flag
globe — globe globe globe
blow — blow blow blow

Choose the right words from the list. Spell them.

The sky is Blue.

We stick things with glue.

At night we go to sleep.

Birds can fly.

I like to play tag.

~~glue~~
~~fly~~
~~blue~~
~~play~~
sleep

Spelling

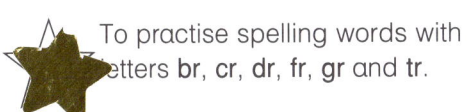

To practise spelling words with letters br, cr, dr, fr, gr and tr.

Words with **br**, **cr**, **dr**, **fr**, **gr**, **tr**

Write the letters **br**, **cr**, **dr**, **fr**, **gr**, or **tr** to spell each word.
Spell the words to finish the sentences.

dr u m  Baby bangs a **drum**.

fr o g  A **frog** can swim.

br i c k  The wall needs one more **brick**.

cr i s p s  I like **crisps**.

gr a s s  The **grass** is green.

tr a i n  The **train** is late.

Read each word. Cover it. Then spell it on your own.

brown **brown**   tree **trees**   crab **crab**

drive **drive**   draw **draw**   cry **cry**

front **front**   fruit **fruit**   green **green**

drink **drink**   bring **bring**   truck **truck**

Spelling

Words with double letters

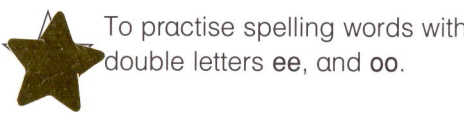
To practise spelling words with double letters ee, and oo.

Write **ee** or **oo** to complete the words. Spell each word twice, then cover and try to spell again, on your own this time.

tr**ee**   tree   tree   tree

b**oo**t   boot   boot   boot

b**ee**   bee   bee   bee

sh**ee**p   sheep   sheep   sheep

d**oo**r   door   door   door

f**ee**t   feet   feet   feet

b**oo**k   book   book   book

m**oo**n   moon   moon   moon

Write **ee** or **oo**.

m**oo**n   b**oo**k   w**oo**f

Spelling

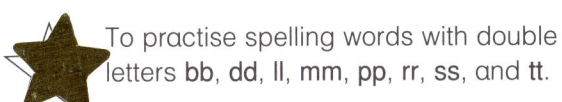

To practise spelling words with double letters bb, dd, ll, mm, pp, rr, ss, and tt.

Words with double letters

Choose letters from this list to spell the double letter words:
bb, **dd**, **ll**, **mm**, **pp**, **rr**, **ss**, **tt**. Spell each word twice.

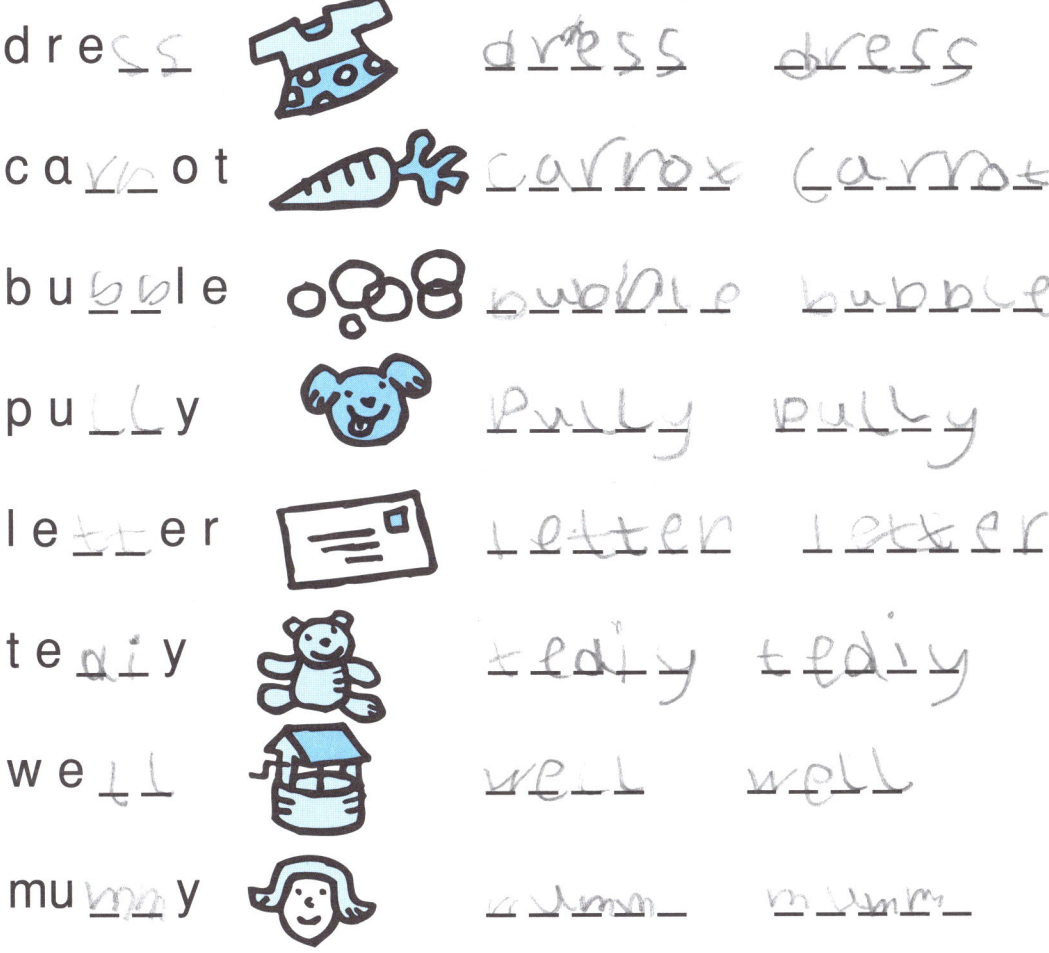

dre ss   dress   dress

ca rr ot   carrot carrot

bu bb le   bubble bubble

pu ll y   pully pully

le tt er   letter letter

te dd y   teddy teddy

we ll   well well

mu mm y   mummy mummy

Underline the double letter words.

Little Tommy Tucker sang for his supper.

Betty Botter bought a bit of better butter.

Spelling

Words with qu and kn

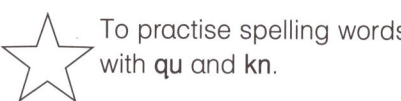
To practise spelling words with qu and kn.

Practise spelling **qu** words. Write each word twice.

quiet _____ _____   quack _____ _____

quite _____ _____   quiz ____ ____

quarter _____ _____

Write **qu** to spell these words. Draw a picture for each one.

 __ilt   __een

Write **kn** to spell the words. Spell each word twice, then cover and try to spell again, on your own this time.

__ ee   ____ ____

__ it   ____ ____ ____

__ ot   ____ ____ ____

__ ife   _____ _____ _____

__ ight _____ _____ _____

Spelling

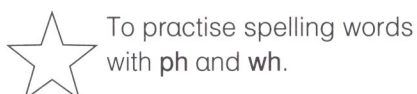 To practise spelling words with ph and wh.

Words with **ph** and **wh**

Write **ph** to spell the words. Spell the words twice more. Match the words to the pictures.

_ _ o t o   _ _ _ _ _   _ _ _ _ _

g r a _ _   _ _ _ _ _   _ _ _ _ _

_ _ o n e   _ _ _ _ _   _ _ _ _ _

Write **wh** to spell the words. Choose and spell each one to finish the questions.

_ _ o   _ _ a t   _ _ e r e   _ _ e n   _ _ y   _ _ i c h

_ _ _ _ _ of these buns do you want?

_ _ _ _ is the answer?

_ _ _ _ _ are you going to?

_ _ _ is hiding?

_ _ _ do balls bounce?

_ _ _ _ is your birthday?

17

Spelling

Words with oa and ow

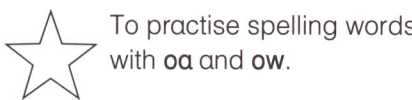

To practise spelling words with oa and ow.

Write **oa** or **ow** to spell the words. Spell each word twice, then cover and try to spell again, on your own this time.

c<u>oa</u>t — coat coat coat

b<u>ow</u> — bow bow bow

g<u>oa</u>t — goat goat goat

cr<u>ow</u> — crow crow crow

s<u>oa</u>p — soap soap soap

Choose the right words from the list. Spell them.

~~mow~~ ~~grow~~ flow loaf boat oat ~~float~~ ~~slow~~ ~~cloak~~

The opposite of fast is slow.

mow the grass.

The opposite of to sink is to float.

Flowers grow in the garden.

Red Riding Hood always wore a red cloak.

Spelling

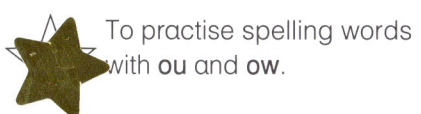 To practise spelling words with **ou** and **ow**.

Words with **ou** and **ow**

A word is hidden in each row of the word puzzle.

The picture clues will help you find the words.

Draw a circle around each word.

Spell the words you find.

 clown

 shout

house

n	c	l	o	w	n	n	o	c	e
x	s	o	s	h	o	u	t	a	s
p	h	o	u	s	e	n	a	e	t
a	o	u	d	o	w	n	m	x	u
f	r	o	b	d	t	o	w	e	l
b	f	r	o	w	n	g	y	r	c
r	k	l	r	o	u	n	d	t	e

down

_ _ _ _ _

_ _ _ _ _

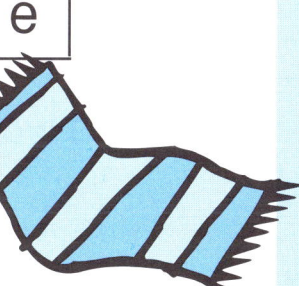

_ _ _ _ _

Spelling

Spelling words with ai

To practise spelling words with ai.

Write **ai** to spell the words. Spell each word twice, then cover the words and try to spell again, on your own this time.

r_ai_n   rayn rayn rayn
h_ai_r   hair hair hair
p_ai_nt   paynt Paynt Paynt
sn_ai_l   snayl snayl snayl
t_ai_l   tayl tayl tayl
st_ai_rs stayrs stayrs stayrs
s_ai_lor sayl__ sayl__ sayl__
f_ai_ry   fayry fayry fayry

Tick the words that are spelled correctly.

gain ✓   agen ✓   fail ✓   pait ✓   wait ✓   chain ✓
gane ✓   again ✓ faile ✓ pain ✓   wate ✓   chaim ✓

20

Spelling

☆ To practise spelling words with different **ea** sounds.

Spelling words with ea

Rearrange the letters to spell the words correctly.
Spell each word twice more.

f e a l   ____   ____ ____

s a e   ___   ___ ___

e a d b s   _____   _____ _____

These **ea** words have a different sound.

d e a h   ____   ____ ____

b d r e a   _____   _____ _____

a e p r   ____   ____ ____

Choose **ea** words from the list to finish the story.

| leader   east |
| treasure |
| heavy   read |

One day pirates went looking for _____. Captain Cutlass was the _____. He ____ his map. "Turn to the ____ at the tree," he said. "Now dig!" They found a big box. It was very _____.

   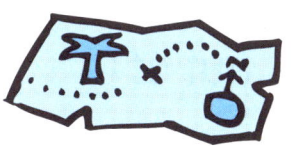

Spelling

Words that end with **ay**

To practise spelling words with **ay**.

Read the words with **ay**.

| bay day hay lay pay ray say way |

Do the letter sums to make more words with **ay**.
Spell them twice more.

pl + ay = Play Play Play

del + ay = delay delay delay

cl + ay = clay clay clay

pr + ay = Pray Pray Pray

rel + ay = relay relay relay

j + ay = Jay jay jay

Choose one of the new words to finish each sentence.

I ran in the relay race.

I saw a jay in the woods.

I made a pot out of clay.

22

Spelling

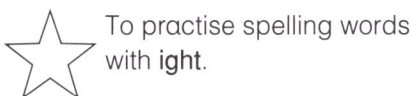
To practise spelling words with **ight**.

Words that end with **ight**

Spell the words to complete the crossword.
All the words end with **ight**.

1 night is the opposite of day.

2 If you can see, you have sight.

3 The balloon popped. It gave me a fright.

4 Tie the rope. Pull it tight.

5 What is on TV tonight?

6 I have two hands, left and right.

Spelling

Adding ing

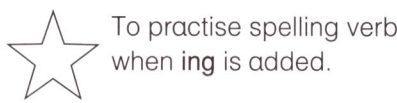 To practise spelling verbs when ing is added.

Add **ing** to spell these words. Spell them twice more.

talk + ing = **talking** _____ _____

sing + ing = _____ _____ _____

read + ing = _____ _____ _____

For these words you must add an extra letter, so **I hop** becomes **I am hopping**.

sit + ing = _____ _____ _____

run + ing = _____ _____ _____

skip + ing = _____ _____ _____

In words that end in **e**, the **e** is left out when **ing** is added. For example **I hope** becomes **I am hoping**.

make + ing = _____

share + ing = _____

dance + ing = _____

bite + ing = _____

write + ing = _____

Spelling

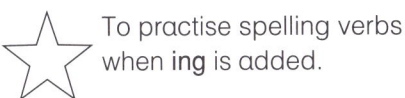
To practise spelling verbs when **ing** is added.

Adding **ing**

Add **ing** to these words. Spell them twice more.

win *winning* _____ _____

hum _____ _____ _____

cut _____ _____ _____

get _____ _____ _____

slip _____ _____ _____

swim _____ _____ _____

take _____ _____ _____

come _____ _____ _____

smile _____ _____ _____

give _____ _____ _____

wave _____ _____ _____

use _____ _____ _____

Spelling

Adding s

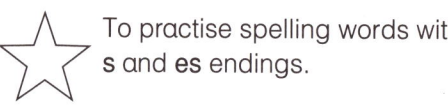
To practise spelling words with s and es endings.

Read the singular words. Spell the plural word for each one. Some plurals are spelled by adding **s**, and some by adding **es**.

plurals with **s**	plurals with **es**
bell _____	fish _____
girl _____	dress _____
toy _____	dish _____
mug _____	watch _____
paint _____	witch _____
apple _____	wish _____
bear _____	bench _____
robot _____	potato _____
plate _____	cross _____
chair _____	tomato _____
rabbit _____	church _____

26

Spelling

 To practise spelling plurals ending **ies**, and plurals that do not follow rules.

Adding s

Spell the plural for the words ending in **y**.

Add **s** for these words

day **days**

play _____

bay _____

boy _____

These words lose the **y** and have **ies** added

baby _____

pony _____

daisy _____

story _____

The plurals for these words do not follow rules.
Tick the correct spelling and spell it twice.

mouse   mouses   mice   ____ ____

leaf   leafs   leaves   _____ _____

woman   women   womans   _____ _____

sheep   sheeps   sheap   _____ _____

man   men   mans   ___ ___

foot   foots   feet   ____ ____

Spelling

Words that rhyme

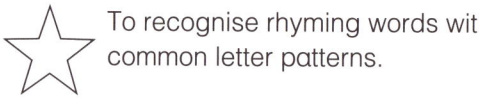 To recognise rhyming words with common letter patterns.

Words that rhyme often have the same letter endings, as in **pan** and **fan**, **sell** and **tell**.

Find a word that rhymes with each of the words below. Choose from the words in the box. Spell it.

wing <u>sing</u>

sack ____

cake ____

hand ____

well ____

kick ____

lend ____

hill ____

gold ____

ball ____

fair ____

| pick |
| hold |
| band |
| send |
| pair |
| make |
| wall |
| sing |
| bill |
| bell |
| back |

28

Spelling

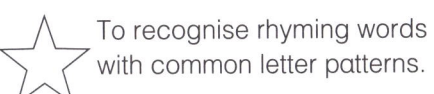

To recognise rhyming words with common letter patterns.

Words that rhyme

Read the poems and underline the words that rhyme.
Spell the words in the rhyme boxes.

Hey, diddle <u>diddle</u>,
The cat and the <u>fiddle</u>,
The cow jumped
   over the moon.
The little dog laughed
   to see such fun,
And the dish ran away
   with the spoon.

_ _ _ _ _ _

_ _ _ _ _ _

_ _ _ _

_ _ _ _ _

Ding dong bell,
Pussy's in the well!
Who put her in?
Little Tommy Thin.
Who pulled her out?
Little Johnny Stout.

_ _ _ _

_ _ _ _

_ _

_ _ _

_ _ _

_ _ _ _ _

29

Spelling

Number words

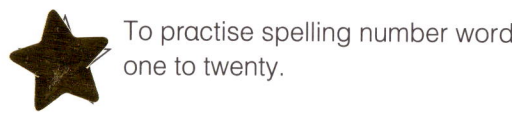
To practise spelling number words one to twenty.

Cover the words and try to spell them on your own.

1 one one
2 two two
3 three three
4 four four
5 five five
6 six six
7 seven seven
8 eight eight
9 nine nine
10 ten ten

11 eleven eleven
12 twelve twelve
13 thirteen thirteen
14 fourteen fourteen
15 fifteen fifteen
16 sixteen sixteen
17 seventeen seventeen
18 eighteen eighteen
19 nineteen nineteen
20 twenty twenty

Spelling

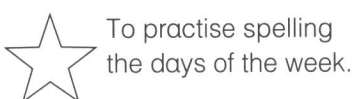

To practise spelling the days of the week.

Days of the week

Rearrange the letters to spell the days of the week.

daySun _Sunday_

Thrusday _____

Mandoy _____

ridayF _____

yasdueT _____

Sutarday _____

Wendesday _____

Spelling

Months of the year

 To practise spelling the months of the year.

Tick the correct spellings of the months of the year and spell them again.

January ✓   Janury   January

February   Febuary   _____

Martch   March   _____

Aprul   April   _____

May   Mae   ___

Juin   June   ____

July   Julie   ____

Augast   August   _____

Septembur   September   _____

October   Octobur   _____

November   Novumber   _____

December   Decenbur   _____

32